W9-AVI-441

AN OVERVIEW OF THE AMERICAN REVOLUTION—
THROUGH
PRIMARY SOURCES

John Micklos, Jr.

Enslow Publishers, Inc.
40 Industrial Road
Box 398
Berkeley Heights, NJ 07922
USA

http://www.enslow.com

Original edition published as *What Was the Revolutionary War All About?* in 2008.

Library of Congress Cataloging-in-Publication Data

Micklos, John.
  [What was the Revolutionary War all about?]
  An overview of the American Revolution—through primary sources / John Micklos, Jr.
      p. cm. — (The American Revolution through primary sources)
  Original edition published as What Was the Revolutionary War All About? in 2008.
  Includes bibliographical references and index.
  Summary: "Provides a general overview of the American Revolution, including the causes of the conflict, major battles, important figures, and how the United States defeated Great Britain and formed a new nation"—Provided by publisher.
  ISBN 978-0-7660-4135-6
  1. United States—History—Revolution, 1775–1783—Juvenile literature. I. Title.
  E208.M46 2013
  973.3—dc23
                          2012015589

Future editions:
Paperback ISBN: 978-1-4644-0193-0   EPUB ISBN: 978-1-4645-1106-6
Single-User PDF ISBN: 978-1-4646-1106-3   Multi-User PDF ISBN: 978-0-7660-5735-7

Printed in the United States of America

082012 Lake Book Manufacturing, Inc., Melrose Park, IL

10 9 8 7 6 5 4 3 2 1

To Our Readers: We have done our best to make sure all Internet Addresses in this book were active and appropriate when we went to press. However, the author and the publisher have no control over and assume no liability for the material available on those Internet sites or on other Web sites they may link to. Any comments or suggestions can be sent by email to comments@enslow.com or to the address on the back cover.

♻ Enslow Publishers, Inc., is committed to printing our books on recycled paper. The paper in every book contains 10% to 30% post-consumer waste (PCW). The cover board on the outside of each book contains 100% PCW. Our goal is to do our part to help young people and the environment too!

Illustration Credits: © Corel Corporation, pp. 18–19, 31; Domenick D'Andrea, courtesy of the National Guard, pp. 1, 3, 4, 13, 30; Enslow Publishers, Inc., p. 9; Independence National Historic Park, p. 38; Library of Congress Geography and Map Division, p. 39; Library of Congress Manuscript Division, p. 21; Library of Congress Prints and Photographs, pp. 5, 11, 22, 36; Library of Congress Rare Books and Special Collections Division, p. 14; Maher / Photos.com, p. 32; Mark Dyson / Photos.com, p. 35; National Archives, pp. 24, 40; Photos.com, p. 16; Shutterstock.com, p. 34; U.S. Senate Collection, p. 28; Valley Forge National Historic Park, p. 27.

Cover Illustration: Domenick D'Andrea, courtesy of the National Guard (Illustration depicts American and British soldiers exchanging fire on Concord Bridge).

CONTENTS

---★---

LOOK FOR THIS SYMBOL **PRIMARY SOURCE** TO FIND THE PRIMARY SOURCES THROUGHOUT THIS BOOK.

Members of the Massachusetts colonial militia fire their muskets at the attacking British soldiers during the Battle of Concord.

CHAPTER 1

⎯⎯⎯ ★ ⎯⎯⎯

A SHOT HEARD ROUND THE WORLD

The church bell in Lexington, Massachusetts, rang an alarm early on the morning of April 19, 1775. It warned that British soldiers, or regulars, were marching toward the town. Paul Revere and other patriots had ridden through the night to sound the alarm: "Turn out! Turn out! The Regulars are out!"[1]

Soon, a small group of armed citizens had gathered on Lexington Green. These were not professional soldiers, like the British regulars. Rather, they were farmers and tradesmen who had joined the local militia unit, pledging to turn out for military service if called upon in an emergency. The militia leader, Captain John Parker, told them to stand ready.

When the British troops arrived, their commander, Major John Pitcairn, ordered the militia to leave. "Throw down your arms! Ye villains. Ye rebels."[2] Greatly outnumbered, the militia slowly began to move away. But then a shot rang out. No one knows who fired it, but more shots followed. The skirmish lasted perhaps two minutes. Eight patriots had been killed. Ten more were wounded. A single British soldier was wounded.

The British troops, who were known as redcoats, marched on toward the town of Concord. They hoped to seize guns and supplies hidden there. They also hoped to capture patriot leaders Samuel Adams and John Hancock. The British wanted to stop what they saw as a growing revolt.

At Concord, a much larger force of militiamen had gathered. British units clashed with the Massachusetts men at a bridge outside the town. Under deadly gunfire, the redcoats fled. After regrouping, they set off for Boston, where British forces were headquartered. Throughout the long march, they were shot at

Night Rider

Before the American Revolution, silversmith Paul Revere was best known for his engraving of the Boston Massacre of 1770. Today, he is remembered for riding through the night to alert people that British troops were marching toward Lexington. "I alarmed almost every house, till I got to Lexington," he later wrote.[3]

The British captured Revere that evening. One soldier, he later recalled, held a pistol to his head and threatened to "blow my brains out."[4] They later released him.

For many years, few people knew about Revere's ride. In 1863, Henry Wadsworth Longfellow published a poem titled "The Midnight Ride of Paul Revere." That poem made Revere famous.

by militiamen hiding inside houses and behind trees and walls. "We were fired on from all sides," wrote one British soldier.[5]

Years later, poet Ralph Waldo Emerson called the battle at Concord "the shot heard round the world."[6] The day's fighting marked the beginning of the American Revolution. But the seeds of the conflict had been growing for decades.

The first permanent English settlement in North America was established in Jamestown, Virginia, in 1607. By 1733, thirteen British colonies stretched from New England to Georgia. Many people in the colonies had never seen England. Yet they continued to see themselves as English. They enjoyed the freedoms of English citizens and were protected by British power. They supported the king.

During the 1760s, however, the ties between Britain and its North American colonies started to weaken. Colonists began to think England had an unfair amount of control over them. They believed they were being denied their rights as English citizens.

Surprisingly, one event that contributed to this belief was a war in which British regular soldiers and American colonists fought side by side against French soldiers and Indians. Among colonists, this struggle for control over North America was called the French and Indian War. The war began in 1754. By 1763, the British side had won. Britain gained control of Canada from France.

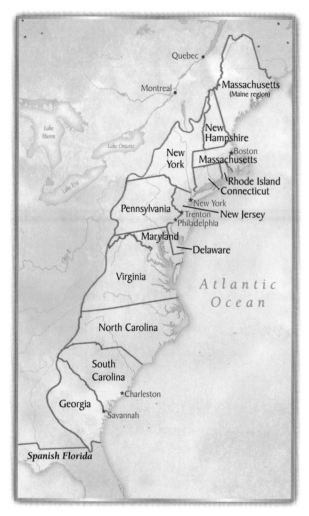

The thirteen colonies stretched along the east coast of North America, from New England to Georgia.

But the war led to several problems between Britain and the American colonies. For one thing, King George III issued a proclamation closing land beyond the Appalachian Mountains to colonial settlers. The Appalachians were on the western frontier of the colonies. The proclamation was a British effort to keep peace with the American Indians. But many colonists did not like it.

Also, England had gone into debt to pay for the war. British officials believed the colonists should help pay some of the war's costs. Parliament, England's lawmaking body, decided to raise money from the American colonies through various taxes. First, Parliament passed the Sugar Act. This law made colonists pay a sum of money for all molasses and sugar brought into the colonies. Then Parliament passed the Stamp Act. It taxed printed material, including books, newspapers, and playing cards.

The colonists were not allowed to vote for members of Parliament. This meant they had no say in how they were taxed. Many believed this was unfair. "No taxation without representation" became a popular phrase.[7] Soon colonists set up a boycott. They refused to buy many English goods.

In October 1765, delegates (representatives) from nine of the colonies met at the Stamp Act Congress in New York City. They said that Parliament had no right to tax the colonies. However, the actions of ordinary people had a much greater impact. Colonists rioted. They attacked tax collectors.

The protests worked. The taxes were repealed, or canceled. Soon, however, Parliament set up new taxes.

The BLOODY MASSACRE perpetrated in King Street BOSTON on March 5th 1770 by a party of the 29th Reg

Engrav'd Printed & Sold by Paul REVERE Boston

Unhappy BOSTON! see thy Sons deplore,
Thy hallow'd Walks besmear'd with guiltless Gore:
While faithless P——n and his savage Bands,
With murd'rous Rancour stretch their bloody Hands;
Like fierce Barbarians grinning o'er their Prey,
Approve the Carnage and enjoy the Day.

If scalding drops from Rage from Anguish Wrung
If speechless Sorrows lab'ring for a Tongue
Or if a weeping World can ought appease
The plaintive Ghosts of Victims such as these;
The Patriot's copious Tears for each are shed,
A glorious Tribute which embalms the Dead.

But know Fate summons to that awful Goal.
Where JUSTICE strips the Murd'rer of his Soul:
Should venal C——ts the scandal of the Land.
Snatch the relentless Villain from her Hand,
Keen Execrations on this Plate inscrib'd,
Shall reach a JUDGE who never can be brib'd.

The unhappy Sufferers were Mess's. SAM¹ GRAY SAM¹ MAVERICK, JAM⁵ CALDWELL, CRISPUS ATTUCKS & PAT⁴ CARR
Killed. Six wounded; two of them (CHRIST⁵ MONK & JOHN CLARK) Mortally

Published in 1770 by Paul Revere Boston

Paul Revere's engraving, "The Bloody Massacre Perpetrated in King's Street," portrayed the Boston Massacre on March 5, 1770. The violent attack resulted in five colonists dead and six more wounded. Crispus Attucks, the only African American to die in the assault, is shown near the bottom of the image.

Boston Massacre

On March 5, 1770, a crowd gathered near the Customs House in Boston. They threw icy snowballs at the British sentries on duty. "You dare not fire," they taunted the soldiers.[8] Then someone in the mob threw a club. It knocked down Private Hugh Montgomery. Getting up, the British soldier leveled his musket and fired.

Soon more shots echoed in the night.

When it was over, five colonists were dead. Six others were wounded.

Many colonists were angry that there were British troops in America. On March 5, 1770, that anger led to deadly violence in Boston. Yet even this event, known as the Boston Massacre, did not lead to war. Five more years would pass before the "shot heard round the world" was fired.

CHAPTER 2

THE WAR BEGINS

On December 16, 1773, an American Indian war cry rang out in Boston. A group of Massachusetts patriots pretending to be Mohawk Indians rushed to the wharf and boarded three ships loaded with British tea. They dumped 342 cases of tea into the harbor. Colonists called this the Boston Tea Party. The lost tea was worth $90,000, a huge sum at a time when the average worker earned less than a dollar a day.[1]

King George III believed that "there must always be [at least] one tax" on the colonies.[2] This would show that England had the right to tax colonists. By 1773, the only British tax the American colonists paid was on tea. And in spite of the tax, English tea was cheap.

A group of angry colonists dump chests of tea into the Boston harbor on December 16, 1773. This act of defiance came to be known as the Boston Tea Party.

Still, colonists thought the tax was unfair. They decided to boycott English tea. The Boston Tea Party took matters further.

When news of the dumped tea reached England, King George was outraged. He encouraged Parliament to pass laws called the Coercive Acts. These acts aimed to coerce, or force, the people of Boston into changing their behavior. The British banned town meetings in Massachusetts. They closed the port of Boston.

They also sent more soldiers to the city, and colonists had to allow these soldiers to live in their homes. The colonists believed these measures violated their rights as British subjects. They called them the Intolerable Acts. Intolerable means unbearable or impossible to accept.

In September 1774, more than fifty delegates from the colonies met in Philadelphia to discuss what to do. This meeting was called the First Continental Congress. The delegates issued a declaration of American rights. It called on Parliament to repeal the Intolerable Acts. To put pressure on Parliament, the colonies agreed to stop importing or using any goods from Great Britain.

But the delegates to the First Continental Congress made clear that they still considered themselves "his majesty's most loyal subjects."[3] Like most Americans at this time, the majority of delegates wanted to mend ties with England.

For his part, King George seemed eager to put the rebellious colonists in their place. "Blows must decide whether they are to

PRIMARY SOURCE

King George III wears his military uniform in a portrait from about 1800. The British king was eager to end the colonists' rebellion.

be subject to this country or independent," the king wrote in November 1774.[4]

Meanwhile, everyone waited to see what would happen in Boston. Tensions mounted. Then came the battles at Lexington and Concord in April 1775. War had begun.

Soon, more than ten thousand American militiamen from throughout New England took up positions outside Boston. They kept the British troops bottled up in the city. That was not too difficult. Boston lay at the end of a peninsula. It was connected to the mainland by a narrow strip of land. The redcoats did not dare try to march across that narrow land.

But when the Americans built dirt walls on a hill on nearby Charlestown Peninsula, the British had to do something. From Breed's Hill, the Americans could fire cannons at Boston. So on June 17, British troops tried to storm the hill. "Don't fire until you see the whites of their eyes!" the American troops under the command of General Israel Putnam and Colonel William Prescott were ordered.[5] American gunfire turned back two British attacks. Finally, the British took Breed's Hill and nearby Bunker Hill. But more than a thousand British soldiers were killed or wounded in the fight, which came to be known as the Battle of Bunker Hill.

Just days before the battle, the Second Continental Congress had created an official army. It was called the Continental Army. Congress chose George Washington of Virginia to lead it. He had fought in the French and Indian War. General Washington took charge of the army at Cambridge, Massachusetts, in July 1775.

Many members of Congress still hoped for peace. In early July, Congress sent the Olive Branch Petition to King George III.

The Battle of Bunker Hill, a British victory, resulted in many casualties for both sides. The death of colonial militia general Joseph Warren was immortalized in this 1786 painting by John Trumbull, who was alive at the time of the battle.

Sizing Up the War

British Advantages

- England had the largest navy in the world. At the start of the war, the thirteen colonies had no navy at all.

- The British army had well-trained troops and seasoned generals. The British also hired thousands of German professional soldiers. The Continental Army had little battle experience.

- Many American colonists supported the British.

American Advantages

- It took months to travel by ship from the colonies to England and back. This made it difficult for British leaders to respond to developments in America.

- The Americans fought with passion because they fought for freedom and to protect their land.

- The Americans received support from Britain's enemies, such as France.

PRIMARY SOURCE

In Congress

George Washington

This document issued by the Continental Congress in early July 1775 commissioned George Washington as commander-in-chief of the newly-created Continental Army.

The king turned down this appeal to restore good relations with the American colonies.

Many British generals had considered the American rebels an "untrained rabble" they could easily defeat.[6] By the end of 1775, however, some had begun to realize they were in for a long fight.

CHAPTER 3

★

A DARING DECLARATION

After nearly a year of war, many colonists still hoped to mend ties with England. Then, early in 1776, a writer named Thomas Paine published a pamphlet called *Common Sense*. It called for independence. England had rejected "every quiet method for peace," Paine said, so "for God's sake, let us come to a final separation."[1] In less than three months, 120,000 copies of *Common Sense* were sold. More and more people began to support the cause of American independence.

In July, the Second Continental Congress prepared a document that made the point even clearer. Thomas Jefferson drafted the document—the Declaration of Independence. "All men are created equal" and have certain rights that can never be taken away, the Declaration stated.[2] These rights include "Life, Liberty, and the pursuit of Happiness."[3] If a government destroys or even fails to protect these rights—as Great Britain had, according to the Declaration—the people may set up a new government.

After much debate, twelve colonies voted for independence on July 2. (New York officially voted for independence two weeks later.) Delegates formally adopted the Declaration of Independence on July 4, 1776.

Now there was no going back. The colonies had officially cut ties with Great Britain. They had proclaimed themselves "free and independent states"—the United States of America.[4]

But declaring independence was one thing. Beating the enemy on the battlefield would be harder. Although the Continental Army had succeeded in forcing the British out of Boston in March 1776, the Americans lacked organization, supplies, and training. Many Continental soldiers signed up for just a few months. When their time was up, they simply went home.

The Declaration of Independence, drafted by Thomas Jefferson, formally declared the colonists' independence from Great Britain.

During the summer of 1776, General Washington was trying to defend New York from a much larger British force. When the British attacked on Long Island, the Americans were quickly beaten. Washington's army was nearly trapped, but managed to escape across the East River. However, the Continental Army was defeated and forced to retreat again. By fall, the British had captured New York City.

Washington knew that the Americans could not win the war in one huge battle. But they could lose it that way. He aimed to keep the war going by never risking his whole army. He hoped the British would eventually grow tired of fighting.

That outcome seemed hard to imagine in the final weeks of 1776. Throughout November and early December, the British chased Washington's retreating troops across New Jersey. Finally, the Americans crossed the Delaware River into Pennsylvania.

Although they were safe for the time being, the American troops were very discouraged. They had suffered one brutal defeat after another. Many of the troops were due to go home at the end

General George Washington

Brave. Daring. Calm under pressure. These traits made General George Washington an ideal leader for the Continental Army. More than any other single person, Washington won the American Revolution for the Americans.

A wealthy Virginia planter, Washington had fought bravely in the French and Indian War. He was a popular choice to head the Continental Army. His soldiers trusted and admired him. During battle, most generals stayed in back, where it was safe. Not Washington. He often rode into the thick of the action.

of the year. No wonder Thomas Paine wrote, "These are the times that try men's souls."[5]

On Christmas night, Washington led his troops across the Delaware River into New Jersey. After all the soldiers had crossed the river, they began a grueling march to Trenton. Many of the men did not have coats or decent shoes. Major James Wilkinson

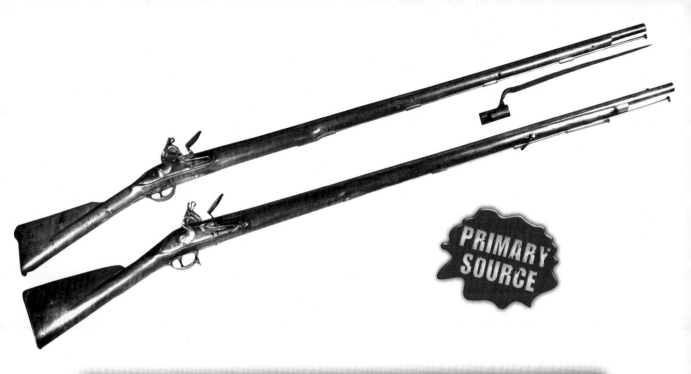

After crossing the icy Delaware River, George Washington's soldiers surprised the British and Hessian troops at the Battle of Trenton. Continental Army muskets, such as those seen here on display at Valley Forge, helped the Americans claim victory in the battle.

wrote that the ground "was tinged here and there with blood from the feet of the men who wore broken shoes."[6]

Around 8 A.M., Washington's army reached Trenton. The town was occupied by a group of German professional soldiers the British had hired. The Americans caught these men, who were called Hessians, by surprise. After a brief but fierce fight, the Hessians surrendered.

General George Washington's bold tactics helped his soldiers defeat the British at the battles of Trenton and Princeton. These great victories gave the Continental Army renewed confidence. This painting of Washington was

Choosing Sides

Not everyone in America supported the cause of independence. Many people believed America should keep its ties to England because the British Empire had helped the colonies grow and prosper. Others did not care one way or the other. They simply wanted to live in peace. Many slaves joined the British army. The British promised them freedom for doing so.

The people who supported the British were called *loyalists* or *Tories*. The people who supported independence called themselves patriots. The British referred to them as rebels.

The Americans killed or captured more than 900 Hessians in the battle. Washington did not lose a single man.

The victory raised the morale of the American troops. Washington decided to strike again. On January 3, 1777, he defeated the British at Princeton, New Jersey.

The battles of Trenton and Princeton helped turn the tide of the war. They made Americans believe they could win.

CHAPTER 4

★

THE WAR DRAGS ON

In June 1777, the British general John Burgoyne invaded New York from Canada. He commanded an army of more than seven thousand soldiers. His plan was to march south to Albany. There, he would link up with British forces moving north along the Hudson River. This would cut off New England from the other states. It might mean the end of the rebellion.

However, Burgoyne's invasion did not go as he had planned. Supplies ran low. A series of battles wore the British army down. The redcoat force Burgoyne expected to meet him never arrived. By October, Burgoyne was outnumbered and trapped.

The surrender of British general John Burgoyne to American general Horatio Gates at the Battle of Saratoga in New York on October 17, 1777, is shown in this painting by John Trumbull.

On October 17, he surrendered to the American general Horatio Gates at Saratoga, New York.

This was a major turning point in the war. A large British force had been defeated. France became convinced that America could win the war. Soon King Louis XVI decided to join the fight against

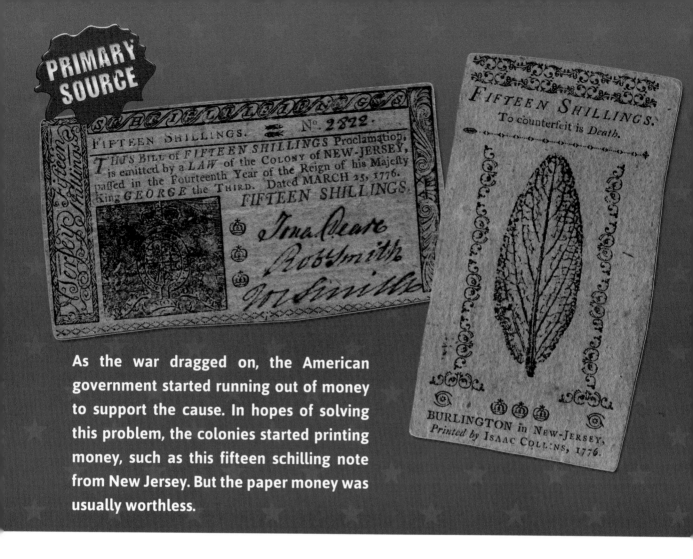

FIFTEEN SHILLINGS. No. 2822.

THIS BILL of FIFTEEN SHILLINGS Proclamation, is emitted by a *LAW* of the COLONY of NEW-JERSEY, passed in the Fourteenth Year of the Reign of his Majesty King GEORGE the THIRD. Dated MARCH 25, 1776.

FIFTEEN SHILLINGS.

FIFTEEN SHILLINGS.
To counterfeit is Death.

BURLINGTON in NEW-JERSEY,
Printed by ISAAC COLLINS, 1776.

As the war dragged on, the American government started running out of money to support the cause. In hopes of solving this problem, the colonies started printing money, such as this fifteen schilling note from New Jersey. But the paper money was usually worthless.

England, the longtime enemy of France. The French had a strong navy. They could provide money, arms, soldiers, and supplies.

However, not all the news was good for the patriots. In August 1777, a British fleet sailed up the Chesapeake Bay. About fifteen thousand troops under the command of General William Howe landed at Head of Elk, Maryland. Howe began marching his army toward Philadelphia. George Washington quickly moved more than twelve thousand men to block Howe's advance.

On September 11, the British and Continental armies fought each other along a creek about 30 miles southwest of Philadelphia. At the Battle of Brandywine, the Americans were defeated. Washington still told Congress that he would "take every measure in my power to defend" Philadelphia.[1] But Howe could not be stopped. On September 26, the British marched into the rebel capital. Congress had fled the city a week earlier.

The British army spent the winter in comfortable quarters in and around Philadelphia. Washington set up camp at Valley Forge. His men huddled in makeshift huts. Many did not have warm clothes. Some did not even have shoes. Food was scarce. During the harsh winter of 1777–1778, as many as 2,500 American soldiers died at Valley Forge. That was about one in four men in Washington's army. Despite the hardships, the Continental Army became a much better fighting force during the winter at Valley Forge.

A reconstructed soldiers' hut at Valley Forge. In Washington's winter camp, the soldiers tried to keep warm in their makeshift huts. The hungry and poorly-supplied troops struggled through the winter, but came out of it better trained and more prepared.

In June 1778, the British decided to abandon Philadelphia. They were worried about being trapped in the city if French forces arrived to aid the Americans. The British marched back to New York.

On July 9, 1778, a French fleet did arrive to help the Americans. But this did not quickly change the situation.

Journey of the Liberty Bell

To many patriots, the Liberty Bell in Philadelphia served as a symbol of the Revolution. The bell had been rung in July 1776 to announce the Declaration of Independence. As British troops approached Philadelphia in late 1777, the patriots vowed to keep it safe. They carefully packed the bell. Then they shipped it in an army baggage train to Allentown, Pennsylvania. There they hid it in a church basement. The bell was returned to Philadelphia on June 27, 1778.

PRIMARY SOURCE

The war dragged on. This created problems for both sides. The British struggled to maintain support for the war at home, and the Americans had trouble finding money to pay for the war effort. Which side would crack first?

CHAPTER 5

VICTORY AND FREEDOM

During the first years of the American Revolution, most of the fighting took place in the North. And the British won most of the battles. They also captured the major cities of New York and Philadelphia. But they were unable to stamp out the rebellion.

British general Henry Clinton decided to try a new strategy. The British would invade the southern colonies. Clinton knew that many people there were still loyal to the king. He hoped these loyalists would join the fight against the American rebels.

In December 1779, Clinton set sail from New York City with about 8,500 British troops. By May 1780, these troops had captured Charleston, South Carolina. About five thousand

Continental soldiers and patriot militiamen were taken prisoner. After this, bands of South Carolina loyalists began attacking their patriot neighbors. Patriots struck back. The fighting was savage.

Clinton's strategy seemed to be working. He decided to return to New York. He left General Charles Cornwallis in command in the South. In August 1780, Cornwallis won a big victory at Camden, South Carolina.

Now the only resistance to the British in South Carolina came from a few small patriot militias. These groups struck quickly and without warning. Then they disappeared into nearby woods or swamps. Leaders such as South Carolina's Francis Marion were good at this type of warfare. The British could never catch Marion. They nicknamed him "the Swamp Fox."[1]

In December 1780, a new American general took over in the South. Nathanael Greene did not have many men. But he had a plan. He would get Cornwallis to chase him through the rugged countryside of North Carolina. This would tire out the British soldiers.

PRIMARY SOURCE

Nathanael Greene, shown in this 1783 portrait by Charles Willson Peale, led a small force to many victories over British general Charles Cornwallis in North Carolina.

Greene's plan worked. After two months, the redcoats were exhausted. Greene decided to fight them at Guilford Courthouse, North Carolina. On March 15, 1781, Cornwallis lost more than one-quarter of his men in the battle there.

Cornwallis knew he could not hold North and South Carolina now. He decided to march into Virginia. Eventually, he moved his troops to Yorktown on the coast. That proved to be a mistake. George Washington had joined his army with French forces led by General Rochambeau. In late August, the American and French troops began a fast, six-week march from New York to Yorktown. They hoped to trap Cornwallis.

In this 1781 engraving, the French Navy attack British forces by sea while the Continental Army bombard the stronghold from land during the siege of Yorktown.

In the meantime, a French fleet under Admiral de Grasse arrived at the mouth of the Chesapeake Bay. Cornwallis now had no way to escape.

In late September, the American and French forces began attacking Yorktown. Day after day, they bombarded the British with cannon fire. Finally, on October 19, 1781, Cornwallis surrendered his entire army of more than eight thousand men.

This is page one of the original copy of the U.S. Constitution.

It took a month for the news to reach England. At first, King George III wanted to keep fighting. But Parliament would not support the war any longer. Yorktown would be the last major battle of the American Revolution.

Nearly two years passed before the war officially ended. Finally, on September 3, 1783, the Treaty of Paris was signed. England recognized the independence of the United States.

But the new nation struggled. The government was weak. The states did not always work together.

In 1787, delegates from all of the states except Rhode Island met in Philadelphia. They hoped to solve these problems. After months of debate, the delegates finally wrote the United States Constitution. The Constitution accomplished what the delegates hoped. It created a government that has helped the United States stay free and strong for more than 225 years.

TIMELINE

1764–1773

The Sugar Act of 1764 places a tax on molasses and sugar. Many colonists boycott English products in protest.

The Stamp Act is passed in 1765. In response, colonists call the Stamp Act Congress.

On March 5, 1770, five Americans are killed in the Boston Massacre.

On December 16, 1773, patriots throw crates of tea into Boston Harbor.

1775

On April 19, Lexington and Concord mark the first battles of the American Revolution.

On June 17, the British Army wins a costly battle at Breed's Hill and Bunker Hill.

George Washington takes command of the Continental Army at Cambridge, Massachusetts, in early July.

1776

The Continental Congress adopts the Declaration of Independence on July 4.

George Washington captures the Hessian outpost at Trenton, New Jersey, on December 26.

1777

On January 3, Washington defeats the British at Princeton, New Jersey.

The British defeat Washington's troops at the Battle of Brandywine on September 11.

On September 26, the British march into Philadelphia.

Timeline

The British general John Burgoyne surrenders his army at Saratoga, New York, on October 17.

In December, Washington's troops arrive at Valley Forge for the winter.

1778

In February, France becomes the first official ally of the Americans.

American and British troops battle at Monmouth Court House, New Jersey, on June 28. The last major battle in the North ends in a draw.

In December, the British capture Savannah, Georgia.

1779

In September, John Paul Jones wins a sea battle off the coast of England. He becomes the patriots' first naval hero.

In September and October, a patriot effort to recapture Savannah fails.

1780

On May 12, the British capture Charleston, South Carolina.

On August 16, the British smash the Continental Army in the South at the Battle of Camden, South Carolina.

Francis Marion leads a small patriot militia in attacks against the British army and their loyalist supporters.

1781–1783

On March 15, 1781, the Battle of Guilford Courthouse in North Carolina cripples the army of General Cornwallis.

Cornwallis surrenders at Yorktown, Virginia, on October 19, 1781.

On September 3, 1783, the Treaty of Paris is signed, officially ending the war.

The British recognize American independence.

CHAPTER NOTES

CHAPTER 1: A SHOT HEARD ROUND THE WORLD

1. William H. Hallahan, *The Day the American Revolution Began: 19 April 1775* (New York: William Morrow, 2000), p. 23.
2. Ibid., p. 30.
3. "Letter from Paul Revere to Dr. Jeremy Belknap," *Documents of the American Revolution,* © 2000, <http://www.historycentral.com/Revolt/battleaccounts/lexington.html> (August 19, 2006).
4. Ibid.
5. "A British Account of Concord Bridge," *Documents of the American Revolution,* © 2000, <http://www.historycentral.com/Revolt/battleaccounts/lexington3.html> (January 3, 2007).
6. Ralph Waldo Emerson, "Concord Hymn, Sung at the Completion of the Battle Monument," July 4, 1837," *Bartleby,* n.d., <http://www.bartleby.com/42/768.html> (January 3, 2007).
7. John Ferling, *A Leap in the Dark: The Struggle to Create the American Republic* (New York: Oxford University Press, 2003), p. 42.
8. "The Boston Massacre," *The Freedom Trail,* n.d., <http://www.thefreedomtrail.org/visitor/boston-massacre.html> (November 27, 2007).

CHAPTER 2: THE WAR BEGINS

1. Alan Axelrod, *The Complete Idiot's Guide to the American Revolution* (New York: Alpha Books/Penguin, 2000), p. 92.
2. John M. Thompson, *The Revolutionary War* (Washington, D.C.: National Geographic Society, 2004), p. 18.
3. "The Articles of Association; October 20, 1774," *The Avalon Project at Yale Law School,* 2008, < http://avalon.law.yale.edu/18th_century/contcong_10-20-74.asp> (January 15, 2007).

4. Thomas Fleming, *Liberty! The American Revolution* (New York: Viking, 1997), p. 88.
5. Axelrod, p. 128.
6. Gordon S. Wood, *The American Revolution* (New York: Modern Library/Random House, 2002), p. 54.

CHAPTER 3: A DARING DECLARATION

1. Thomas Paine, *Common Sense,* July 4, 1995, <http://www.ushistory.org/Paine/commonsense/singlehtml.htm> (January 8, 2007).
2. U.S. Declaration of Independence.
3. Ibid.
4. Ibid.
5. Thomas Fleming, *Liberty! The American Revolution* (New York: Viking, 1997), p. 214.
6. David Hackett Fischer, *Washington's Crossing* (New York: Oxford University Press, 2004), p. 210.

CHAPTER 4: THE WAR DRAGS ON

1. John Buchanan, *The Road to Valley Forge: How Washington Built the Army That Won the Revolution* (New York: John Wiley & Sons, 2004), p. 252.

CHAPTER 5: VICTORY AND FREEDOM

1. Ronald W. McGranahan, "Brigadier General Francis Marion: 'The Swamp Fox,'" *The American Revolution Home Page,* n.d., <http://www.americanrevwar.homestead.com/files/MARION.HTM> (August 21, 2006).

GLOSSARY

boycott—To refuse to buy or use a product, often as a form of protest.

coerce—To make someone do something by force.

constitution—A document creating a government. The U.S. Constitution outlines the government's powers and lists some of the people's rights.

declaration—A formal statement. The Declaration of Independence announced America's break from England.

Hessians—German professional soldiers hired by the British.

intolerable—Impossible to accept or bear.

massacre—The act of killing a number of people, especially when they are helpless or not resisting.

militia—Citizens who train as soldiers from time to time and are available to serve in an emergency.

Parliament—The legislative, or lawmaking, body of Great Britain.

petition—A formal written request.

primary source—A document, text, or physical object which was written or created during the time under discussion.

proclamation—An official public announcement.

repeal—To withdraw or cancel a law.

representation—In government, the practice of having members of an assembly or lawmaking body act on behalf of other citizens.

Tories—Americans who supported the British during the American Revolution.

FURTHER READING

Books

Fleming, Thomas. ***Everybody's Revolution: A New Look at the People Who Won America's Freedom.*** New York: Scholastic Nonfiction, 2006.

Freedman, Russell. ***Washington at Valley Forge.*** New York: Holiday House, 2008.

Huey, Lois Miner. ***Voices of the American Revolution: Stories From the Battlefields.*** Mankato, Minn.: Capstone Press, 2011.

Marston, Daniel. ***The American Revolutionary War.*** New York: Rosen Publishing Group, 2011.

Murphy, Jim. ***The Crossing: How George Washington Saved the American Revolution.*** New York: Scholastic Press, 2010.

Internet Addresses

PBS—Liberty!: The American Revolution
 <http://www.pbs.org/ktca/liberty/>

The Declaration of Independence
 <http://www.ushistory.org/declaration/document/index.htm>

INDEX